My World

My World

Poems of Life & Growth

Janie Emerson

Cover Photo by Janie Emerson

Copyright © 1999, 2025 Janie Emerson.
All rights reserved. This book or any portion
thereof may not be reproduced or used in any
manner whatsoever without the express written
permission of the publisher except for the use of
brief quotations in a book review.

ISBN: 978-0-9716320-6-6
Cover photo by Janie Emerson
Book design by Janie Emerson
Printed in the United States of America.

JEM Enterprises
La Jolla, California

ShamrockWisdom.com

DEDICATED TO

That special child
in all of us.
May she live and
thrive forever.

CONTENTS

Introduction

THIS IS LIFE

This is Life	3
My Flower World	5
Humming Bird	7
Butterfly	9
Joy	11
Excitement	13
Wishes	15

WHO AM I ?

Who Am I ?	19
The Child	21
Order	23
Seeing	25
We Dream Together	27
Your Day	29

THE PATH

The Path	33
Your Spirit	35
Waiting For Grandpa	37
For My Love	39
Regrets	41
Footsteps	43
I Walk Alone	45

CONTENTS

THE KEY

The Key	49
New Beginnings	51
Flips	53
Now	55
Freedom	57
About The Author	59

INTRODUCTION

My World allows us the space to view and create the world we want from the world we have.

There is much in today's world that is positive, fun, and exciting. Tap into that.

Use your creative power. Connect with your inner child. Create that special world just for you now.

Make your world for you always.

BLOSSOM - GROW - THRIVE

THIS IS LIFE

THIS IS LIFE

Our hearts beat
    With love and hope.
Our minds cling
    To thoughts and dreams.

Our souls sing
    With joy and life.
Our spirit warms
    To beauty and peace.

This is life –

My Flower World

A sacred place of
      beauty, joy,
           and color

A place to play.
A place for rest.

A special place of
      safety, dreams,
           and peace.

My flower world
Is just for me.

HUMMING BIRD

Your
      Irridescence
           Lights the
                  Bough.

You flit -
      You glisten -
           You float -
                You fly . . . .

BUTTERFLY

It floats so brilliantly
      and effortlessly it moves.

It anoints each flower
      with colors so they glow.

It wraps all in beauty
      and in joy it gently goes.

JOY

energy
    enthusiasm
        electricity

sunshine
    seashore
        smiles

companions
    competition
        contentment

enjoy
    sing
        celebrate !

EXCITEMENT

Embrace
>   the joy of
>   >   life
>   >   >   With every breath !!

Enjoy
>   the quiet of
>   >   life
>   >   >   Create it now !!

Excitement
>   is all of these
>   >   and
>   >   >   So much more . . . .

WISHES

A Wish is -
    Wispy,
        Warm,
            and Loving.

Our Wish is -
    Lovely,
        Light,
            and Healing.

My Wish is -
    Happy,
        Heartfelt,
            and True.

Wishes are –
    Friends
        Forever
            and Ours.

WHO AM I ?

WHO AM I?

Others say
> I intimidate.
I perceive
> they prevaricate.

Now is the time
> to reveal the TRUTH ...
And uncover this
> finally as a ruse !

Who am I ?
> I am me . . . .

THE CHILD

Happy and carefree,
Dancing through the flowers.
With gleeful joy.

Happy and carefree,
Loving every blade of grass,
With unconscious love.

Happy and carefree,
Playing with birds in the yard,
With total glee.

Happy and carefree,
Loving all life,
With open arms.

Happy and carefree
          Always –

ORDER

I give and receive

    The two of these –

        A perfect balance.

SEEING

I see now with eyes anew

Where there was lack,
    I see is now full

Where there was limit,
    I see no bounds.

My eyes now see –
    They see anew.

WE DREAM TOGETHER

We dream together
For joy and life.

We dream together
To heal from strife.

We dream together
For love this life.

We dream together
For paths of light.

We dream together
To Him for right.

We dream together
Our dreams give life . . . .

YOUR DAY

There are days to sing,
>   Days to dance with great joy.

There are days to rest,
>   Days of peace to enjoy.

There are days to work,
>   Days to create and employ.

The best days are to laugh,
>   To love and dream with joy.

Your days are the special ones,
>   Days to live and totally enjoy.

THE PATH

THE PATH

I walk this path alone
With weary steps I trudge.
My heart is stone,
My feet are lead.
My body bowed with dread.

Where is the light
To guide me clearly on ?
Why so dark
This path I walk alone ?

I walk this path in faith
With prayful steps I move.
My heart believes,
My dreams are clear,
My being filled with love.

Here is the light
It guides me from within.
Now so bright
This path I walk to home.

YOUR SPIRIT

We miss your spirit,
    Walking the beach,
        Creating the cures,
Walking through life . . . .

We miss your spirit,
    Its touch forever,
        A touch for all,
Empowering us all . . . .

We miss your spirit,
    It was so free,
        It is now here,
It is ours forever . . . .

WAITING FOR GRANDPA

They are all crying -
I wait for Grandpa,
      He will make it right.

Everyone is wearing black -
But Grandpa wears blue.
      He will make all right.

They are all somber -
I want Grandpa to play.
      He always makes it right.

Everyone says good-byes -
But Granpa lies so quiet.
      He will make all right.

All is dark and quiet -
I wait for my Grandpa
      He is now white light.

FOR MY LOVE

We stood there, just long enough,
    in sweet warm wind
        that never did notice us.

We stood there, just long enough
    for me to think first
    there was something
        completely human about
        kissing your forehead.

And that not to have done it
    would have been
        like not telling the truth ....

REGRETS

I watched as he turned and moved to go -
    Our souls still touch,
        Still merge as one . . . .

Years lived for others, now long gone.
    Regrets tightly locked inside
        Never to be found.

I waited, turned and slowly moved to go -
    He watched and wondered
        "Will it be ours now?"

This love so strong it lights our lives,
    Its power illumines all,
        Ignites and entwines.

He blows a kiss, sighs and turns -
    I touch our souls,
        We dream of one . . . .

FOOTSTEPS

I walk each day alone -
    In solitary pain.
They said they'd always be there;
    I only now remain.

I walk the beach alone -
    With tears upon my face.
My memories my sole companion;
    They match my heavy pace.

I walk my lonely way -
    As my dreams depart.
Were are the joys and hugs of yore
    To lift this aching heart.

The beach is solitary now -
    In quiet it remains.
No footprints upon the sand,
    The water masks all pain . . . .

I WALK ALONE

I walk alone -
I know many people,
Have many friends,
      and
            I walk alone.

My soul feels solitary.
I touch others with love -
They are healed,
      and
            I walk alone.

I give to all -
I reach out to cheer.
So who is beside me
      when
            I walk alone ?

I walk with love -
My soulmates my true companions.
Love is the healer,
      now
            I walk not alone.

THE KEY

THE KEY

The key is
      A special gift,
           Do not lose it from disuse.

Use it,
      Enjoy it,
           It opens all of life.

Pass it on –

NEW BEGINNINGS

Time to build,
    To square our lives –
        No more shoulds,
            musts or,
                oughts . . .

Only our pure priorities
    Only simple sharings –
        For now is
            our solid
                New Beginning . . . .

FLIPS

Flip the card,
Turn the page,
This side is done
>   On to the next stage !

No more surrogates,
No more roles.
This acting is done
>   Now is time to live ....

NOW

I am more open,
> More flexible in
> My beliefs and words.

From now on –

Life is more than
> Black and white,
> Right and wrong.

It is also pink –

Enjoy the pink . . . .
> Enjoy it now . . . .
>> Enjoy it always . . . .

FREEDOM

Freedom to see,
Freedom to be
    Way up in a tree
        And free to be me ...

Freedom to dream
Freedom to scream
    Ideas are a beam
        To light up the scene ...

Freedom to be
    Just really me !

ABOUT THE AUTHOR

JANIE EMERSON

Janie Emerson is the author of the successful *Appreciate Each Day, The Magic of Me, Inner Magic, Guided By Animal Angels, Walking With Angels,* and *My Special Girls.*

Janie has written for newspapers and won national awards for her poetry. Her poems have been recorded and published.

The inspiration for Janie's writings comes from life. Janie's work gives balance, insight, and focus to life's events. Her intent is to empower and to enhance your life through these poems.

Janie is a respected consultant and acclaimed speaker. She has been an advocate for women owned businesses nationally, and an active community leader.

Janie was born and raised outside Philadelphia, on the Main Line. She and her husband Bob live in La Jolla, California with her beloved Westies.

Janie is currently working on two new exciting projects.

www.ingramcontent.com/pod-product-compliance
Lightning Source LLC
Chambersburg PA
CBHW062113290426
44110CB00023B/2804